W9-CBR-937

STARTING POINT

A Parent's Journal for Dreaming

This journal belongs to:

Dynamic Catholic

© 2019 Dynamic Catholic Institute

All rights reserved.

No part of this book may be used or reproduced in any manner whatsoever without permission except in the case of brief quotations embodied in critical articles or reviews.

The Scripture quotations contained herein are from the Catholic Edition of the Revised Standard Version Bible, copyright © 1965, 1966 by the Division of Christian Education of the National Council of the Churches of Christ in the U.S.A., and are used by permission.

Prayers adapted from Fr. Liam Lawton's *The Hope Prayer*

Dynamic Catholic®, Be Bold. Be Catholic.®, the-best-version-of-yourself®, are registered trademarks of Dynamic Catholic.

Design by Doug Beyer, Ben West, and Ashley Wirfel

ISBN: 978-1-63582-128-4

FIRST EDITION

10 9 8 7 6 5 4 3 2 1

The Story Behind STARTING POINT

This project began with a dream: to create the best baptismal preparation experience in the world. For the millions of parents who will experience this program, we hope we have delivered on that dream.

Hundreds of people have poured their time, talent, and expertise into STARTING POINT. It is the result of years of research, development, and testing. To everyone who has contributed in every stage of the process: Thank you! May God bless you and reward you richly for your generosity.

Beyond the enormous talent contributions, others have been incredibly generous with their money. STARTING POINT was funded by a group of passionate donors. It will now be made available at no cost to every parish in the United States. This is one of the many ways that this program is unique.

Everything great in history has been accomplished by people who believed that the future could be better than the past.
Thank you for believing!

Now we offer STARTING POINT to the Church as a gift, hopeful that it will help parents raise great children with the grace of God.

Note: Individuals and couples cited as examples in this work are real. However, their names and circumstances have often been modified to preserve their privacy.

Special thanks to: Jack Beers, Katie Beers, Donald Carson, Claire Darnell, Megan Everett, Deacon Leo Gahafer, Peter Herbert, Anita Hunt, Deacon Charles Iner, Fr. Jonathan Meyer, Mark Moore, Lindsey Schrock, and Fr. Bob Sherry.

Designed by: The Dynamic Catholic Design Team
Principal Designers: Doug Beyer, Ben West, and Ashley Wirfel

Table of Contents

PART 1

Dreams for Your Child

WELCOME!

Nothing could have prepared me to become a father. No matter how many books I read or couples I spoke to, the day my first daughter was born was a "turn my world upside down" kind of day.

One night, shortly after she was born, I was begging her to stop crying and go to sleep. As she wailed, so many thoughts ran through my mind—everything from "Will I ever sleep again?" to "Does she know I have no clue what I am doing?" I didn't know if it was day or night. I looked like I had just lost a wrestling match with a panther. I hadn't showered in who knows how long. A small part of me started to wonder if the hospital takes returns: "Honey, where's the receipt?"

But after an hour of crying, she finally closed her eyes and fell asleep in my arms. Everything changed. She looked so peaceful and beautiful. And it hit me: I was her daddy.

In that moment I realized there is nothing I would not do, no distance I would not travel to protect this little girl.

Watching her sleep, I thought about who she might become. I began to dream about her life. What would her laugh sound like? What ideas would keep her up at night? What would it be like to show her the world? How could I help her become a good person?

In those precious minutes, I experienced the wonder of being a new parent—overwhelming responsibility mixed with surges of love and hope. You've probably experienced that, too.

While you might be exhausted, a bit overwhelmed, worried about your own abilities as a parent, or concerned about the world your child was born into, you have also probably surprised yourself. You might be surprised by your ability to function on so little sleep. Or surprised by how willing you are to sacrifice for someone you have just met. Or surprised by how much you could love a little boy or girl.

While nothing can fully prepare you to become a mom or a dad, you can prepare to become a great mom or dad.

And that is precisely what this dream journal is all about.

God never goes back;
he always moves forward . . .
God always wants our future to
be bigger than our past.

MATTHEW KELLY

Your Child's Name

The Story Behind the Name

You did not choose this name randomly. There is a reason for it; it was a choice. Your child's name is deeply personal, as it should be. Every name has a story behind it.

Tell your story here:

You Have Nine Years

When he was nineteen years old, Usain Bolt began training with his coach, Glen Mills, for the Olympics. Three years later, after thousands of hours of workouts, a strict diet, and an unwavering 24-7 focus, Bolt arrived at the Beijing Olympics. He stepped up to the block for the 100-meter sprint.

The gun sounded. The runners were off. And 9.69 seconds later, Bolt crossed the finish line, setting an Olympic record and winning the gold medal.

Just 9.69 seconds. Before most of us even had time to blink, the race was over. After all the training, all the sacrifice, all the blood, sweat, and tears, it was over in a mere 9.69 seconds.

Parenting is like that. It will be over before you know it.

Before you know it, you'll be waking your son up for his first day of high school. You'll feed him breakfast and kiss him good-bye. As he leaves, you will pray he makes good friends.

Before you know it, your daughter will come home crying. She didn't get the part in the play. Her best friend did. You will pray this motivates her instead of breaking her.

The day is coming when your baby will be out in the world making his or her own decisions. You'll want to help. You'll want to be a positive influence in those biggest moments. And you can be. Just not in the way you think.

Your primary concerns right now are keeping your infant alive and getting a full cycle of sleep again. You probably aren't thinking about all the BIG STUFF just yet. After all, you've got 18 years to influence your child, right? Nope.

Actually, you have nine years. That's 3,285 days—life's equivalent of 9.69 seconds.

During those first nine years of life, your child develops her decision-making patterns. Her moral compass is formed. Her spiritual foundation is poured. And helping her in that process is one of the most important responsibilities you have as a parent. You have nine years—3,285 days.

By the time a child reaches the age of nine, her personality, what she believes about the world and about God, her perception of self, love, and relationships— all of that is already largely set.

By the time your child gets to middle school and high school, in the moments when she has to make a decision, either she will be prepared or she won't. She will either have the tools and the confidence to make great decisions or she won't. As much as she will be helped by the conversations you have with her when she is a teen, her decisions will depend largely on how you parent in the first nine years of her life.

Imagine what 3,285 days of excellent parenting can do! You've got nine years, starting now.

DISCUSS

Moral Compass

You have nine years to pour your child's spiritual foundation and to help your child develop her moral compass.

Does this surprise you? Discuss this idea and write down your thoughts here.

READ

Do You Dream?

Wilma had a difficult start to her life.

Born prematurely, she contracted pneumonia, scarlet fever, and polio all before the age of four. She survived, but doctors doubted she would ever walk again.

But Wilma was no ordinary four-year-old.

Day after day, year after year, for eight years, she dedicated herself to the dream of walking again. The prescribed physical therapy regimen was demanding and painful. But Wilma never quit. She poured every ounce of energy into the pursuit of her improbable dream.

By twelve Wilma wasn't just walking. She was running. In fact, she was the fastest kid in the school . . . including the boys. But she wasn't ready to stop there. Instead, she had something bigger in mind. This time she trained to compete.

After eight more years of dedication, she was Olympic fast. So fast that she set the Olympic record for the fastest times in the 100-meter and 200-meter races, making Wilma Rudolph the fastest woman in the world. Not bad for a girl who was told she would likely never walk again.

Years later, when asked how she was able to achieve the improbable, she simply said, "The doctors told me I would never walk again. My mother told me I would. I believed my mother."

Wilma Rudolph's mother taught her to be a person of possibility. People of possibility rise above the shadow of their real self into a shining example of what the human person is actually capable of. People of possibility spread joy, wisdom, and energy to everyone who crosses their path. When you encounter a person of possibility, you are lovingly challenged to pursue the greatness you were created for.

While not everything in life can be overcome with hard work and perseverance, everyone can become a person of possibility.

Becoming a person of possibility is not something that happens by magic. Those who become people of possibility are those who harness two of God's greatest gifts: free will and our ability to dream.

From the moment we are born we are endowed with free will. This gift means our choices are our own. We get a say in what our future will be like. The type of person we become is our choice.

The second gift is our ability to dream. What would the world look like without someone like Dr. Martin Luther King Jr., who dreamed of a better future? What would the world be like without people who could look into the future and see things that no one else can see? People who dream change the world.

Do you dream? Do you set aside time to think about the life you want for yourself, for your marriage, and for your child? It's OK if you don't. That's why you're reading this book. But if you do, how big are your dreams? And do you make choices to support them? Or do you just hope they will somehow come true?

When you dream, you look into the future and see a bigger and better reality. Then you can come back to the present and work to make that future a reality. Best of all, you can teach your child to do the same.

Teach your child to look into the future and see something amazing. Challenge him to work toward that amazing future. Encourage him to persevere when he meets obstacles. Do all this and he will become a person of possibility. He will live a life of greatness.

Look into the future and imagine what kind of parent you want to be. Envision what kind of person you want your child to be. Imagine what kind of family you want to create. Then come back to the present and use your free will to collaborate with God to make that future a reality.

The Ultimate Dream

If you could dream just one dream for your child, what would it be?

Recently, I shared dinner with a man who had donated to the organization I was working with. His achievements in business are admirable. After dinner, the conversation changed.

"Do you know why I give to your ministry?" he asked.

"Because there is something missing in my life. I give money because it affords me the opportunity to meet the people at your organization. There's something about the way you live that is special and rare. You make me want to be better.

"I tell you this because you are young and perhaps it will be of some use to you. I am a very wealthy man. I have more cars than I could ever use, and more money than I could ever spend. I can get whatever I want . . . but I have no peace. Peace is what I want. And the funny thing is, I would give everything I have, the things I have spent my whole life building, for just a little peace. As a little boy I had it, but now as an old man, I have no peace."

His words were tragic. His parents would have been proud of his success but broken by his words. They would have examined their own lives to see where they might have fallen short.

When you look into the eyes of most people you meet today, you will see clouds and storms, anxiety and restlessness. Rarely will you see the calm, peaceful waters of a life well lived.

Great lives are not built by doing and having. A great life comes only by becoming—that is, by spending a lifetime choosing to become a-better-version-of-yourself each day, and asking God to help you do just that.

You were created by God to become the-best-version-of-yourself, your most loving, most generous, most peaceful self. It's the essential purpose of life. If you are a-second-rate-version-of-yourself, does it really matter how successful you are or how good your health is?

Ultimately, peace is the fruit of knowing that you are spending your life on a worthy purpose—that each day you are able to love more than the day before, that you are becoming a better person, that you are responding to the gentle whisper of God calling you to inspire and improve the lives of others. We are not here exclusively to do something, but to be and become someone.

You aren't the only one created by God to become the-best-version-of-yourself and to live a great life. Your child is, too.

You couldn't have a better dream for your child than for her to become the-best-version-of-herself. It is the ultimate dream for those we love. It is the only path to peace.

TIP: Create a poster with these words and hang it in your child's room to inspire greatness each day.

Or go to **DynamicCatholic.com/Poster** to view one available there.

(Check out the boy's version of this poster on the following page. You can see the girl's version on page 23).

I AM THE *son*
OF A GREAT **KING.**
He is my father
AND MY GOD.
THE WORLD MAY PRAISE ME
OR CRITICIZE ME.

IT MATTERS NOT.

always at my side,
GUIDING AND PROTECTING ME.
I DO NOT FEAR
because
I AM HIS.

READ

Your Dream List

When parents begin to seriously think about their dreams, those dreams emerge rather quickly. Most people discover that it is not that they don't have dreams for their child, but that they have so many, they can't possibly pursue them all.

This is a great moment to stop and ask yourself: What are my dreams for my child?

People who dream—who share their dreams and try to live them each day—are simply more engaged in their children's lives. Their children grow up with a sense that their parents want what's best for them. And couples who learn to dream together have marriages that are longer, fuller, and happier. Now is your time to dream.

As you progress through this journal you will encounter ten dream categories, each with questions to inspire your dreams and help you capture them on paper. They are designed only to help you start your dreaming. You will think of other dreams beyond these questions.

There are no right or wrong answers. Work with your spouse. Write quickly. Don't think too much; don't analyze or edit yourself as you make your list. Write everything down, even the ones you feel are foolish (these are often the best dreams!). Your answers don't have to be definitive. They will change over time, but it is still important to write them down now; it will help you as you venture through the rest of your life.

This is your dream list. This is your North Star. Let these dreams guide your decisions. Take steps to achieve them. And follow them into the future of happiness and greatness that God desires for you and your family.

Now is your time to dream.

Your Dream List 1: *Emotional*

- What kinds of friendships do you dream for your child?

- What kind of relationship would you like with your child when he is in his teens?

- What would you like your relationship to look like when he is an adult?

Dreaming is Contagious
[example dreams]

I want my child to have a close-knit relationship with
my parents and extended family.

I would like my child to grow up surrounded by a
supportive community of family and friends.

REFLECT

Your Baby Now

Being a parent is life-changing, but the early months can be tough (understatement of the century!). They are also precious and fleeting. Think about the things you want to remember about your child's infancy.

Jot a few of them down here.

Mom:

Dad:

I AM THE *daughter*
OF A GREAT **KING.**
He is my father
AND MY GOD.
THE WORLD MAY PRAISE ME
OR CRITICIZE ME.

IT MATTERS NOT.

HE IS WITH ME,
always at my side,
GUIDING AND PROTECTING ME.
I DO NOT FEAR
because
I AM HIS.

Every Parent's Dream

She looked at the list of names in the program. His turn was coming soon. She took off her heels and climbed onto the folding chair. She was not going to miss seeing this moment.

Suddenly, the boy's name was called. He walked across the stage. He shook the hand of the principal. Tears of joy slipped down her cheeks. Memories began flashing through her mind.

When her son was born, he rarely cried or fussed, laughed or smiled. If he wasn't eating or sleeping, he just sat there nearly motionless—except when he would hear the sound of his mother's voice. If he was being held by someone else and she came into the room, his head would turn in the direction of her voice and he would smile. She loved that about him. It made her feel so special.

She remembered the day he came home from school crying. The kids at school had made fun of how slowly he read in class. His face was wet with tears. She promised she would spend thirty minutes each night helping him become a better reader. He agreed. And look at him now!

Her mind turned to when he was sixteen. She had just discovered that he had lied about where he was the night before. She was furious. Honesty was the most important thing in their household and he knew that. They argued for an hour before she sent him to his room. They both said things they wish they hadn't. That night, when she went to bed, she found a note on her pillow from her son. "I'm sorry I lied. I won't do it again. I love you." She still has the note.

She came back to the present. When she finally saw her son after the ceremony, he was standing in a large group of his classmates. When he heard her voice, he pushed his way through the crowd and ran to her. They embraced. He whispered, "I wouldn't be here without you, Mom. Thank you."

As he walked away, she knew he didn't need her anymore. He was strong, courageous, and kind. She knew he would go into the world and place his talents and enthusiasm at the service of God and his fellow human beings. She knew he was ready for life.

Certainly she was proud of her son. The day brought her great joy. Her heart was filled with gratitude for the gift of being his mom. Most of all, she experienced a deep sense of satisfaction—the kind that only comes to a parent who can say with complete honesty, "I did my best and gave it my all."

So much is going to happen in your life. Your journey as a parent is just beginning. You have hopes and dreams for your child. But in the end, when you imagine the big moments in his or her life—graduation, first job, marriage, kids—and you know you have done everything you can to lead your child to a great life, can you really imagine a better feeling?

REFLECT

When are you at your best?

TIP: When you take time to think about the moments you are the-best-version-of-yourself, you can learn a lot. Is it when you're reading a good book, when you're serving someone else, when you're well rested, when you're with certain people, or when you've had time alone in the classroom of silence?

Mom:

Dad:

When are you at your worst?

TIP: Think about the things, people, and situations that prevent you from being the-best-version-of-yourself. Maybe it's social media, your phone, TV, your job, a toxic relationship, or when you're tired or hungry. Knowing what is getting in the way can help you avoid these things. Being honest about them with your spouse will help you both tremendously.

Mom:

Dad:

Your Dream List 2: *Intellectual*

- How will you help inspire a love of learning in your children?

- If your child could speak an additional language, what would it be?

Dreaming is Contagious
[example dreams]

I want to read on a daily basis with our child.

I would like our family to have regular puzzle-and-pizza nights.

I hope to expose my child to a variety of areas of knowledge.

Delivery Room

Watch the video, answer the questions to the right, and discuss additional thoughts.

DynamicCatholic.com/DeliveryRoom

Talk About the Video

Dream Writing Session: The parents started their dream journals in the video. Now it's your turn. Take 5 minutes to write down as many dreams as possible.

Dream Prompts: If you could go on one dream trip with your family, what would it be? What kinds of spiritual habits would you like to establish? Do you want physical fitness or healthy diets to be important to your family? What will you do to encourage learning outside of school? How will your children know the importance of saving? Are there any traditions you want to establish around holidays, birthdays and other important days? Describe the character of the man or woman you would like your child to marry. Or the person you want your child to become when he or she is 25.

What surprised you most about this video or the dream writing session?

Was it easy or difficult to think of dreams for your family?

Under what category do most of your dreams fit (financial, spiritual, educational, etc.)? What categories seem lacking?

More of Your Thoughts:

READ

Your Dream Is God's Dream

Your dream for your child to become the-best-version-of-herself and to live a great life is God's dream, too.

Fortunately, God doesn't just tell us his dream for our lives—he shows us the way. Virtue is the tool he gives us to live out that dream.

God guides us to becoming the-best-version-of-ourselves. It's impossible for your child to experience greatness without virtue.

Given the choice between an impatient child and a patient child, which would you pick? How about between an arrogant child and a humble child? A lying child and an honest child?

Easy, right? We all want patient, humble, honest children. Why? Because we've never met an impatient, arrogant, dishonest, happy person. And no one enjoys living or working with a dishonest person.

Patience, humility, honesty—these are all virtues. You won't read about it in a newspaper or see it in an ad, but virtue is the only path to happiness. Virtue is God's big, bright, blinking neon sign pointing to the-best-version-of-yourself, saying: happiness this way!

The Catechism defines virtue as "a habitual and firm disposition to do good" (1833). To become good and to do good—that is virtue. Here's another way to think of it: Virtue is the choice to not be a giant, self-centered jerk.

Truth is, you know virtue when you see it. There's a reason why common virtues transcend religion, culture, and time. These are qualities such as honor, kindness, courage, discipline, compassion, generosity, and wisdom.

As a parent, you can't force your child to live a great life. You can't choose virtue for her. But you can recognize the wisdom of God. You can identify growing in virtue as the key to a great life. And you can choose to create an environment that celebrates virtue each day.

READ

Do As I Do

Like her daddy, my older daughter loves saltine crackers. She used to ask for them all the time. Usually, we gave her one. One time, though, I told her she had to wait for dinner. She lost her mind. Because we want her to learn patience, I did not give in. In fact, I scolded her. The next day, when I was stuck in traffic, I lost my mind. In that moment it hit me. My daughter received more from Daddy than just her love of saltine crackers.

Here's the thing. No one is born virtuous. But we all want to be virtuous (that's the longing for happiness you're always feeling). Living virtuously is something you seek out and acquire through continual practice. You learn to play guitar by practicing guitar. You learn to be virtuous by practicing virtue.

The most effective way to celebrate virtue in your home is to let your children witness you practicing it. Yes, it's great to affirm your son when he is kind, courageous, and honest. Yes, it's important to introduce your daughter to role models who are patient, generous, and full of self-control. But unless you walk the walk, your encouragement will seem shallow and hypocritical. In other words, practice what you preach.

So practice virtue. Practice it openly in front of your children. If you fail, let your child know you failed and let him learn from that. If you're impatient with your spouse, let your child see you apologize and express what you wish you would have done differently.

One of the great things about the virtues is that they are all interconnected. When you grow in one, the others naturally improve as well. You can't become more patient without growing in kindness, love, and every other virtue. So don't worry about doing too little; don't try to do too much. Simply start by trying to grow in one virtue and then go from there.

You can make growing in virtue as important to your family as eating healthy or getting good grades.

And remember, God's dream is your dream. You are not alone in this. He is here to help you along the way.

Don't worry that children never listen to you; worry that they are always watching you.

ROBERT FULGHUM

REFLECT

Your Child's Description of You

When your child is twenty-five years old, how would you like him to describe you as a parent?

TIP: Be honest with yourself. Pick ten words you hope your child will use to describe you as a parent.

Mom:

Dad:

Your Dream List 3: *Character*

- In two to three sentences, describe your child at age eighteen. What kind of character does she have? Is she patient, caring, driven? What are her goals in life? What does she value most? What are the three words you want most to describe her?

- Now fast-forward to your child at age thirty-five. In two or three sentences describe what she is like. What are her goals? What does she value most? What are three words you want most to describe her?

Dreaming is Contagious

[example dreams]

I want my child to be kind and polite.

I want our family to be known by our community and
neighbors as generous and friendly.

I would like our family to be welcoming to guests.

For the day we accept that we have chosen to choose our choices is the day we cast off the shackles of victimhood and are set free to pursue the lives **we were born to live.**

Matthew Kelly

READ

The Culture's Dreams

You have dreams for your child. God has dreams for your child. And the culture has dreams for your child, too.

But the culture doesn't care about your dreams or God's dreams. It doesn't care whether your child becomes the-best-version-of-himself. The culture's idea of being successful is to be rich. The culture's idea of happiness is pleasure. The culture's idea of greatness is power.

Consider this. In 2017, Mattel, the manufacturer of Barbie and Hot Wheels, spent more than $370 million advertising to convince children their lives would simply not be complete without a doll or a toy car. Sony, Microsoft, and Nintendo spend hundreds of millions in market research to understand the most effective way to develop the next addictive video game.

Every day, the culture invests huge amounts of money to influence what your child does, what he has, and what he thinks he needs. The culture doesn't really care who your child becomes.

But you do care. In fact, you care deeply.

The culture knows that whoever deeply wants to have the most influence over your child will have the most influence over your child. But you have the advantage here. You have the opportunity to spend more time with your child than the culture does—especially in those crucial first nine years.

44

Greatness doesn't happen by accident. Your child won't stumble upon it. That's why the culture is so intentional and aggressive in its approach.

The only way to overcome the influential power of the culture is to get really intentional. You have the advantage here. You get to make choices for your child and your family that the culture does not. Be intentional. Invest.

The most effective way to guide your children toward a virtuous life is to live one yourself. After all, children are far more likely to emulate what they see as opposed to what they hear.

So the question becomes, who will win? Who is going to be more intentional with your child? You or the culture?

Your Dream List 4: *Creative*

- What hobby or sport would you like to encourage your child to grow and develop?

- In what ways do you hope to expose your child to different kinds of people, places, art, culture, and music?

Dreaming is Contagious
[example dreams]

I want our children to be involved in at least one
physical activity outside of school.

I would like our family to take monthly "field trips"
to local museums and shows.

I want to be sure my child has sufficient amounts of free time to
explore, imagine, and develop his creativity on his own.

REFLECT

Is the culture already winning in your life?

TIP: Take time to think about how you might be bringing the negative culture into your home. Do you watch TV shows that prevent you from being the-best-version-of-yourself? Do you impulsively buy things that you feel like you need (and regret later)? Do you put your career ahead of your family or your faith?

Mom:

....

....

....

....

Dad:

....

....

....

....

Prayer of a Mother

Lord
I have counted each day waiting
I have whispered new names each night
I have held this child forever

I have dreamed dreams
Beyond my imagining
That come to life in the
Tiny fingers that wind around my thumb

Whatever this child is
And will become
May he know the wisdom of Your Temple days
May he lift the wounded with Your healing way
May his heart be humble should he stray

When your mother let you go
Did she walk the dusty roads forever in her heart
Following You with love

Or did she learn to trust
Even when You walked that hill
And spread your arms for me
And all humanity?

Help me place my life, my flesh, my child
Into Your care, Your arms
Mind him for me
Mind him well

Then one day, Lord
He can tell his child
Of you and of love
As well

Your Dream List 5: *Financial*

- **What do you want your child's relationship with money to be?**

- **What does financial freedom look like to you?**

Dreaming is Contagious
[example dreams]

I want to teach my child how to save money.

I want to pay for my child's education so that she does not have long-term student loan debt.

I want my child to learn how to work for and earn money.

READ

The Road to Excellence

At Dynamic Catholic we are obsessed with excellence. We've studied Olympic champions, titans of industry, world leaders, and great saints in search of a common pattern. And we've discovered they all seem to begin in a similar way.

Whether it's Frank Sinatra, Lebron James, or Mother Teresa, those who achieve greatness begin by establishing who they are and what they want to achieve. They examine the present by defining their needs, talents, desires, strengths, and weaknesses. Then they look to the future. They envision where they want to go and what it takes to get there. This allows them to uncover the gap between who they are and who they dream of becoming.

Once they know who they are and where they are going, they simply start walking. What matters is not how big or small that first step is, but rather simply beginning forward momentum.

The STARTING POINT Parenting Preparation Inventory was created specifically to help you follow this pattern.

The STARTING POINT Parenting Preparation Inventory is one of a kind. Until now, one has never existed. It is designed to be a conversation starter for you as you set out on the journey of parenting, and it was created specifically for you—to help you recognize patterns and implement strategies to achieve excellence in parenting.

It does this in two major ways:

1) **It helps you love intentionally.** How your child experiences love from you has massive ramifications for his life (just like how your parents loved and parented you has had a huge impact on your own life).

2) **It encourages you and your spouse to become a dynamic parenting team.** Taking the inventory together allows you to gain a deeper understanding of where your spouse is coming from, your expectations of each other, and how each of you expects to show love to your child. Every wife has expectations for what type of father her husband will be, just as every husband has expectations for what type of mother his wife will be. Very simply, the inventory sparks conversations to help the two of you get on the same page.

Complete the inventory, answer the questions to the right, and discuss additional thoughts with your spouse.

DynamicCatholic.com/ParentingPrep

DISCUSS

The Inventory

Take the STARTING POINT Parenting Preparation Inventory together, then discuss what you've learned. What are three things that surprised you most in doing the inventory? What did you learn that you didn't realize before about yourself and your spouse?

DISCUSS

Your Childhood

Talk with your spouse about your childhood.

- **What was it like to be a child in your family?**
- **What was the best part of your childhood?**
- **What do you wish you could change about your childhood?**

Prayer of a Father

Lord
Lord, You have now given me
the privilege Of my own family
Help me to accept with humility this sacred gift

May I be gentle and strong,
Knowing right from wrong
May I be firm yet fair
May my wife find in me a companion for life
A true friend, A kind listener
May my children know
protection, affection, direction

May I open for them the book of knowledge
The secret doorway to adventure
May the child in me always
accompany the child in them

May I hold them in times of fear
May I dry the eyes that cry soft tears
May we journey together through many years

Lord, may they know You because of me
Your consoling compassionate way
Woven through life each day

May I be silent when I need to hear
Affirm, and gently steer
The anxious heart to a place of calm

Lord, may I be blessed in my children
May my wonder never cease
May I find with self-acceptance
The gift of inner peace

May I rest with quiet contentment
And make this silent prayer
Father of all Fathers
Guide our earthly way

Amen.

DREAM LIST

Your Dream List 6: *Psychological*

- If you could suspend fear, what activity would you try?

- How will you and your spouse handle discipline in your family?

- Are there any fears you'd like to overcome (and avoid passing on to your child)?

Dreaming is Contagious
[example dreams]

I want to screen movies to be sure they are
appropriate for my child's age.

I would like to build trust so that my child discusses openly
and regularly any fears that he is facing.

READ

The Crucial Habit

Standing in the sprawling baby bottle aisle trying to make a choice is a humbling experience. Just doing an internet search for "baby bottles" brings me to my knees. There are thousands of them. Low flow, high flow. Clear, colored. Every shape and material known to man. And this is just one decision among thousands you'll need to make.

As a parent on the front lines, it's easy to get lost in the details. But really, when you think about it, you have one job: to teach your child to make excellent decisions. Not pretty good decisions—excellent ones. That's where the crucial habit comes into play, and here it is:

Place every important decision in the context of this question: Will this help my child become the-best-version-of-herself? Then, as your child grows, the crucial habit is teaching her how to make good decisions for herself by asking her, "Will this help you become the-best-version-of-yourself?"

Implemented effectively, the crucial habit will shape every decision your child makes for the rest of her life.

Asking the question is the crucial habit for a reason: It's effective. Will this help me become the-best-version-of-myself?

At first, you'll ask the question for your child. Should we let our son watch movies at age two, or should we wait? Should we both work, or should one of us stay home? Should we give in to a tantrum, or stick to our guns?

Will this help my child become the-best-version-of-himself?

As your child develops, you will teach him to ask this question himself. When your ten-year-old son comes home from school and says, "Mom, can I watch TV before I do homework?" you can answer, "Will watching TV before doing your homework help you become the-best-version-of-yourself?"

Let's be honest, he will probably answer yes. But the crucial habit gets him to think. It reminds him that a life of greatness is more important than the immediate pleasure brought by watching TV. And it embeds that crucial question in his head for the decisions still to come.

The crucial habit can be difficult to develop. It takes a lot of energy, and it is built slowly over time. But it is powerful. Most important it will equip your child with the process necessary to walk the path of greatness.

61

READ

The One Thing

Superfood has emerged as a trendy buzzword in recent years. It refers to nutrient-rich food that possesses natural "superpowers" to boost well-being.

For example, broccoli is considered a superfood. It's packed with vitamins and minerals to fight disease, exceptionally high levels of vitamin C, and folate to reduce the risk of heart disease, specific cancers, and even stroke. Pretty super, right? One might even go so far as to say super-duper.

What if I told you there's a superfood that reduces the chance your child will engage in substance abuse by 80 percent—would you want to know what that superfood is? If you found out, would you scramble to fill your child's diet with a steady dose of it?

Well, no superfood can do that. But there is one thing you can cultivate in your child that does: Faith in God.

Studies at Columbia University show that when children have a personal relationship with God, it reduces the risk of depression by 40 percent, reduces the chances they engage in risky sexual behavior by 70 percent, and reduces the chance of engaging in substance abuse by 80 percent.

And that's not all.

The National Study of Youth and Religion at Notre Dame and UNC–Chapel Hill found that adolescents with an active personal religious faith were more likely to:

- **have positive attitudes toward themselves,**
- **feel hopeful about their futures,**
- **feel like they had something of which to be proud,**
- **feel happy to be alive, and**
- **enjoy being in school.**

You want what's best for your child. In fact, you dream of what's best for your child. And faith—a relationship with God—can help you achieve it. It is the superfood. It is the one thing.

If you want to maximize that potential power, there is no time to waste. Your child's faith journey starts now.

Your Dream List 7: *Spiritual*

- What's your dream for helping your child develop a deep sense of inner peace?

- Who does God want your child to be?

- What will your daily prayer routine with your children look like?

Dreaming is Contagious
[example dreams]

I would like our family to pray together on a daily basis.

I want to build family worship as a part of our routine.

I want to make helping my child become a-better-version-of-himself a regular part of our conversations.

READ

The Help of a Great Friend

When each of our two daughters was baptized, dear friends gave us a framed picture of Jesus smiling and holding small children. My wife and I hung those pictures, one in each of our girls' bedrooms, right over their beds.

Because of that gift, our daughters grew up each night of their lives with Jesus watching and smiling over them as they slept.

The significance of this gift became clear when SarahAnn, our older daughter, was preparing to leave for college. Our firstborn would be walking into a new season of her life, a season when her parents would not be looking over her shoulder each day. She would go with hopes and dreams and also with fears and worries. Leaving home for the first time changes everything.

On the evening before her departure for school, we all knew this last night together at home represented a lot. The four of us decided to spend the evening together as a family—no friends, no visitors. This was our last night with things the way they were. The next day, we would drive SarahAnn off to college and things would be different. Only three of us would still be at home.

SarahAnn would be setting out on a new adventure. When she came home now, she would be more like a guest and a grown-up. Things would be different. We all knew that.

So on that last night with her at home, we ate dinner together, played games, and just talked. We wanted to savor every bit of this time. Tomorrow things would change, and there would be no going back to the way they used to be.

Finally, SarahAnn got up and said, "I think I am going to go on to bed. Tomorrow is a big day, and I want to get a little sleep to be ready." She went upstairs to her bedroom.

An hour or two later, I said something similar. "Tomorrow is a big day. Since I am the only man in this family, I'll be doing most of the moving and lifting as we take her stuff to school. So I am going to go on to bed and get some rest so I will be ready."

As I prepared for bed, I told my wife, "I think I will check on SarahAnn and tell her good night."

I walked down the hall to our daughter's room and knocked on the door. No answer. I assumed she was asleep, so I slowly opened the door and peeked in.

There she was, asleep on the bed, her arms wrapped tightly around the picture of the smiling Jesus, pulling it close to her chest.

I knew right then. She was going to be just fine.

She knew him. And she knew he held her future. She was ready.

READ

The Church Wants You to Be Happy

You aren't going to be the only influence in your child's life.

Friendship is a powerful thing.

Your child's friends are going to have a profound influence on her life. If you want your child to become generous, you can't be the only generous person in her life. If you want to help her become the-best-version-of-herself, then it's important for you to surround her with people focused on helping to achieve that goal—for her and for themselves.

Now, unfortunately, you can't see into the future and anticipate all the people your child will come across in her life. You can't even know everything there is to know about the neighborhood you live in or the schools your kids will attend.

But you can introduce your child to one great friend who will actively help you realize the dreams you have for your family. There is one friend who can be there for your child, even when you cannot. And there is one friend who will guide her in times of confusion, inspire her in moments of despair, and give her the strength to choose the-best-version-of-herself—even when it isn't popular to do so.

That great friend is the Catholic Church.

The Church, like God, actually wants nothing more than for you to be happy in this life and in the life to come. And the Church points us in the direction of that happiness with its teachings.

For thousands of years the beauty and genius of Catholicism, with the life and teaching of Jesus Christ, has inspired men and women to live a life of greatness.

There are two key differences between those who lead great lives and those who don't. First, those who live great lives have a singleness of purpose that penetrates their lives. Second, they form the habits to help them achieve their goal. Life-giving habits lead to greatness; the Church helps instill those life-giving habits.

When you look outside the nucleus of your family, you will discover no better guide for the journey ahead than the Catholic Church. The Catholic Church isn't perfect—we all have our hurts and our pains; none of us are immune. But in the Church, we are inspired to love one another, teach one another, encourage one another, heal one another, and bear one another's burdens.

You are not alone in this parenting journey. You were made to raise a great child. You can do this. And the Catholic Church can help.

REFLECT

Faith and Family

Answer the following questions on a scale from 1 to 10. Then, write down why you chose that number.

How important was faith to your family when you were growing up?

Mom: 1 2 3 4 5 6 7 8 9 10

Dad: 1 2 3 4 5 6 7 8 9 10

How important is faith to your marraige now?

Mom: 1 2 3 4 5 6 7 8 9 10

Dad: 1 2 3 4 5 6 7 8 9 10

How important would you like faith to be to your own family?

Mom: 1 2 3 4 5 6 7 8 9 10

Dad: 1 2 3 4 5 6 7 8 9 10

Your Dream List 8: *Legacy*

- What ministry or charity will you serve and support as a family?

- What do you want your children to remember about your family and how you interact with others, especially people in need?

Dreaming is Contagious
[example dreams]

I want to provide a Thanksgiving dinner to a
family in need every year.

I want our family to value elderly persons and
visit a nursing home regularly.

I want our family to feel at home in our parish.

*God, grant me the serenity
to accept the things I cannot change;
courage to change the things I can;
and wisdom to know the difference.*

Amen.

REINHOLD NIEBUHR

READ

Our Lives Change When Our Habits Change

Habits are powerful. They help you achieve your (and God's) dreams. Our lives change when our habits change.

Good habits, such as brushing your teeth and getting regular exercise, lead to your health and well-being. Bad habits, such as eating a bag of potato chips and drinking a liter of Coca-Cola each night before going to bed, negatively affect your health and well-being. Simply put, great habits lead to long-term happiness; poor habits do not.

But good routines are difficult to maintain. We all know our lives are better off when we get enough sleep, exercise regularly, and take time for prayer and reflection. Yet, how many of us do those things on a consistent basis?

Even though good routines lead to happiness, we have a hard time doing them because good routines require discipline. And being disciplined is difficult.

The same can be said for raising children. Having routines and set times for play, food, bath, and sleep takes discipline, which makes those routines hard to maintain. But routines are critical to living a life of greatness.

Routines save your life as a parent. Having structure to your day and life will make everything easier. From knowing where the extra soap is to having a specific night-time ritual, routines give a predictability that feels safe to a child and sane to the parents.

Routines also build healthy habits and manners. We wash our hands before we eat. We watch Mommy and Daddy greet each other with a happy hug. We call Grandpa to say good night. We say a prayer before every meal.

One of the best ways to get really intentional about your parenting is to infuse your family life with great routines. Routines are just habits on a schedule. And they are a parent's best friend. Why? Because routines do the following:

- **teach self-control**
- **reduce power struggles**
- **reinforce desirable behavior**
- **produce good results**
- **bind the family together**

And it is important to know there are two habits—two daily routines—that will be bold game changers for your family.

READ

Game-Changer Habit 1: Our Daily Bread

In a study at Columbia University, teens who regularly ate dinner with their parents showed better results in school and physical health. Countless studies demonstrate how consistent family dinnertime bonds the members of a family together and produces a bevy of positive outcomes.

It makes sense. Dinnertime equals face time. Children learn so much of how to live well from the dinner table. But you as a parent learn even more. You learn about your son's day, his friends, what he thinks is funny, what is troubling him, and more.

Dinner is the opportunity to turn off the TV, put the phones away, take a break from the frenzy of life, and spend meaningful time with your child.

Maximizing dinnertime is simple. Go around the table and ask, "What was the high point of your day?" Encourage your child to share one thing that happened during his day. Listen attentively to his answer, ask follow-up questions, and thank him for sharing. And be sure to share some of your own day as well.

Granted, for the first few years of parenthood, dinner is going to be hectic. And right now your baby can't answer you when you ask how her day was. But establish the routine now, because it's going to be difficult to do so when she gets older.

A dinner routine now becomes a bridge to keep you connected to your child all the way to young adulthood.

READ

Game-Changer Habit 2: Our Daily Prayer

When I am spiritually healthy, I am unstoppable. Go ahead, internet, take forever to load my video. I can wait. Go ahead, blue Nissan, drive as slow as you want in the left lane. I've got all day.

When I am spiritually unhealthy, I'm a mess. I break my phone. I honk my horn and yell obscenities. When I am spiritually unhealthy, prayer is the only cure.

Daily prayer is the number one, most important routine you can establish with your family. Nothing else even comes close. If you want your child to choose a-better-version-of-herself each day, it will begin with prayer. Everything else flows from this.

Without prayer, your child will be operating on her own power. It will be like having an eight-cylinder car but using only two. She will still be moving, just not with the same oomph.

With prayer, however, your child's relationship with Jesus will build over time. Prayer works on the soul much like waves come in day after day and slowly change the coastline. Consistent. Steady. Powerful.

Here are two simple ways to pray as a family each day. Whether one minute or ten minutes, the important thing is to just get started (and keep at it).

1. Use the Dynamic Catholic Prayer Process (explained in the following pages) as a family to start or end each day.

2. At the end of the day, gather as a family. Begin your prayer time with the sign of the cross. Next, have each member of the family share one thing he or she is grateful for that day. Then share one intention you would like God's help with (it could be anything from your child's test that week to the healing of a grandparent or peace in the Middle East). End by reciting an Our Father, a Hail Mary, and a Glory Be together.

Your Dream List 9: *Physical*

- **What are your dreams for your family's lifestyle?**

- **What kind of physical activities do you hope your child will enjoy?**

Dreaming is Contagious
[example dreams]

When my child is older, I want to participate
in a 5K run with her every year.

I want to establish healthy eating habits for my family.

I hope to expose my child to lots of kinds of activity so she can find the
ones that give her the most satisfaction and joy.

READ

How to Pray: 7 Simple Steps to a Better Life

I golf about once every three years. When I do, I get absolutely apoplectic whenever I shoot poorly (which is to say, every hole). After bending a few clubs, I vow to never golf again. I have no idea why I expect to be good at something I never do.

Do you pray? Are you good at it? Were you ever taught to pray? Most of us weren't.

Just like with golf or anything else in life, if you were never taught how to do it and you don't practice it, you probably won't be very good at it. This is why Dynamic Catholic developed the Prayer Process—a simple, helpful way to begin having a daily conversation with God.

When you develop the habit of praying this way each day (it only takes a few minutes), you will begin to see significant things happen in your life and your family.

The
PRAYER PROCESS

STEP ONE: GRATITUDE

Begin by thanking God for whoever and whatever you are most grateful for today. You may want to begin with thanking him for his immeasurable love in your life.

STEP TWO: AWARENESS

Think about yesterday. Talk to God about the times when you were and were not the-best-version-of-yourself.

STEP THREE: SIGNIFICANT MOMENT

Ask God what he is trying to say to you today. Talk to him about that.

STEP FOUR: PEACE

Ask God to forgive you for anything you have done wrong and to fill your heart with peace.

STEP FIVE: FREEDOM

Talk to God about some way he is inviting you to change and grow.

STEP SIX: OTHERS

Pray for the other people in your life by asking God to guide them and watch over them. In particular, pray for your child and those people in positions to influence his or her life.

STEP SEVEN: OUR FATHER

Pray the Our Father.

Get wallet size Prayer Process Cards for your family and friends by visiting:
DynamicCatholic.com/Prayer

DREAM LIST

Your Dream List 10: *Adventure*

- If you could plan one life-changing trip for your child, what would it be?

- What little adventures will you try to have with your family?

- How will you incorporate play into your family life?

Dreaming is Contagious

[example dreams]

I want to go on one family vacation together each year.

I would like to take my child to Italy someday.

I want to try new foods with my family and
encourage them to try new things.

READ

God's Dream for Your Marriage

My parents rarely fought in front of us kids. The arguments I do remember were about who would give the other a shoulder massage during a family movie night. To me as a kid, their displays of affection were embarrassing (and a bit icky). As an adult, I realize their affection made a lasting and positive impact on my life and my perception of love.

In the craziness of parenthood, so much time and energy gets spent on things like when to introduce your child to screen time, how to get your kid on a sleep schedule, how to avoid having a picky eater, how to discipline a toddler or a teenager, and so on. These are important topics, but one of the most important things you can do for your child is to love your spouse well. When you love your spouse with everything you've got, living your wedding vows completely, most of that other stuff will take care of itself.

God wants you to have romance. He wants you to have joyful date nights. He wants you to have a wonderful sex life. He wants you to reach the deepest level of intimacy with your spouse. Quite simply, God wants your marriage to thrive.

Husbands, love your wives. Wives, love your husbands. It just may be the greatest gift you can give your child.

For single parents, whatever your circumstances are, being kind and respectful to your child's other parent will make a significant impact on your child. Even in situations of separation or divorce, it is important that both parents are as involved as possible in their child's life. In situations where the other parent is not involved, well-chosen godparents can make helpful contributions to your child's life. Choose godparents who will be present, positive, and inspiring influences in your child's life.

For free, helpful, and ongoing resources to enrich your marriage, check out BETTER TOGETHER.

DynamicCatholic.com/Enrichment

Better Together

Write down five things you love about your spouse.

TIP: The first three months after our first daughter was born, my wife never looked more frazzled. And she never looked more beautiful! I could never tell her this enough. These five things are great reminders when times get challenging (and they will!). Whenever you are arguing or feeling irritated by your spouse, come back to this page and reread your five things.

Mom: The five things I love most about my husband are . . .

1.
2.
3.
4.
5.

Dad: The five things I love most about my wife are:

1.
2.
3.
4.
5.

Prayer for Parents

Loving God
You are the giver of all we possess,
the source of all of our blessings.
We thank and praise you.

Thank you for the gift of our children.

Help us to set boundaries for them,
and yet encourage them to explore.
Give us the strength and courage to treat
each day as a fresh start.

May our children come to know you, the one true God,
and Jesus Christ, whom you have sent.

May your Holy Spirit help them to grow
in faith, hope, and love, so they may know peace,
truth, and goodness.

May their ears hear your voice.
May their eyes see your presence in all things.
May their lips proclaim your word.
May their hearts be your dwelling place.
May their hands do works of charity.
May their feet walk in the way of Jesus Christ,
your Son and our Lord.

Amen.

No Regrets

After our first daughter was born, I often forgot we had a child. The baby would be napping and I would say things like, "Hey! Want to go get some ice cream?" or "Let's go see a movie!"

I'm not perfect. Neither are you. Fortunately, the-best-version-of-yourself does not mean the-perfect-version-of-yourself.

You are going to mess up. You will make mistakes. All parents do. When Jesus was twelve years old, Mary and Joseph lost him for three days. Three days!

God's dream for you as a parent isn't for you to be mistake-free. Rather, it's for you to be regret-free.

God doesn't want you to be filled with regret. He doesn't want you to be haunted by thoughts like, "I wish I had been more intentional earlier" or "I should have done more" or "I could have been more present." He wants you to have the deep satisfaction of knowing that you gave everything you could to raise an amazing child.

He wants to stand side by side with you along this parenting journey. Encouraging you in difficult moments. Inspiring you in your uncertainty. Providing courage when the right thing is the tough thing. And picking you up when you fall. Because in the end, God wants nothing more than to say to you, "Well done, good and faithful servant."

God isn't asking you to be perfect. He simply invites you to do better today than you did yesterday. Be better today than you were yesterday. The-best-version-of-yourself is a great parent! That person is real. He or she is not some impossible dream.

So, dream big and dream often. There are no foolish dreams; only those foolish enough to think dreams don't matter.

Love your spouse and your children. Love them like Jesus loves you.

Welcome God into your life. Invite Jesus into your home. Ask the Holy Spirit for aid. Let the Church walk with you and your children.

You've got this.

PART 2

Baptism & Beyond

CONGRATULATONS!

Welcome to God's family! You're getting your child baptized. Well done!

You've welcomed your child into the world. You're adjusting to this new little person in your family. You're probably learning to live with a lot less sleep and considerably less free time. I'm guessing you never realized just how little you could care about getting dirty while changing diapers. Maybe you've even learned that you indeed cannot die from yawning too often. Perhaps you're holding a screaming infant in your hands right now as you read this (they're beautiful, aren't they?). And there's no doubt you are being stretched in ways you did not expect or could never have imagined.

Your life has massively changed. But you've still made it to Baptism preparation. Great work!

This is a great first step for your child, and for your family. STARTING POINT (this dream journal and the three videos referenced in it, as well as the Parenting Preparation Inventory) is designed to help you take this first step in raising a great child. Because you want a great family.

Deep down we all do.

REFLECT

God's Dream for Your Family

What few people realize is that your yearning for a great family is actually God stirring something deep inside you. Because God wants you to have a great family, too.

Do you have big dreams for your child's life? Are you hoping God will help you have a great family? Or are you here out of obligation to your parents or grandparents? If so, that's OK. Many couples expect little, if anything, from their baptismal preparation experience. I know I didn't expect much when I was getting ready for my first child's Baptism. It's good to acknowledge that you may well be here because you have to be.

Why are you here? You can write down your thoughts here or just talk about it with your spouse, but be honest with yourself for a few moments. Why are you having your child baptized?

READ

Six "I Dos"

When you get married, you make solemn vows. Even in the most secular weddings, like those on your favorite sitcoms, vows are made. And how do weddings end? The bride and groom always say two little words: I do.

When you have a baby, you are given this little person without making any vows or promises. Isn't that odd? The hospital doesn't ask you to make vows. The government and the culture don't require you to make vows. You don't have to make a single promise to be a parent. Not one!

Well, your child's Baptism is that opportunity to make vows. In fact, you have to. It's part of the rite. And unlike on your wedding day, you don't say "I do" once. You say it six times.

Do you reject Satan?
I do.

And all his works?
I do.

And all his empty promises?
I do.

Do you believe in God, the Father Almighty, creator of heaven and earth?
I do.

Do you believe in Jesus Christ, his only Son, our Lord, who was born of the Virgin Mary, was crucified, died, and was buried, rose from the dead, and is now seated at the right hand of the Father?
I do.

Do you believe in the Holy Spirit, the holy Catholic Church, the communion of saints, the forgiveness of sins, the resurrection of the body, and life everlasting?
I do.

God, the all-powerful Father of our Lord Jesus Christ, has given us a new birth by water and the Holy Spirit, and forgiven all our sins. May he also keep us faithful to our Lord Jesus Christ for ever and ever.
Amen.

The greatest trick the devil ever pulled was convincing the world he didn't exist.

UNKNOWN

103

DISCUSS

Baptismal Vows

The first questions of the baptismal vows are about Satan. Discuss these questions below with your spouse and write down what they mean to you.

- **Do you reject Satan, all his works, and all his empty promises?**

- **What are some ways you have seen the Evil One at work in your own life?**

TIP: There's often a modern impulse to avoid "Satan talk." But Jesus spoke regularly about the devil and evil spirits.

104

A little child has no difficulty in loving, has no obstacles to love. And that is why Jesus said: "Unless you become like little children you cannot enter the kingdom of God."

MOTHER TERESA

READ

Five Signs

Baptism is not an end but a beginning. It begins a life-long, joy-filled relationship with God, a relationship marked by his abundance. Your child belongs to him.

The baptismal ritual is not random. Everything about it, including the five major symbols employed, have profound reasons behind them.

Here's a brief overview of those five symbols you will experience during the Baptism.

1. Light

At Baptism, God floods your child's soul with light. Jesus is the light of the world. As a child of the light, your child will receive wisdom to discern between right and wrong, goodness to desire what is good and true, and courage to make excellent choices. In the not-so-distant future, your child will face dark moments filled with doubt, confusion, and fear. Through the light of Baptism, she can dive deep into her own conscience and hear the will of God guiding her to the next right thing. When your child's candle is lit from the Easter candle, rejoice in the gift of the light.

2. Water

Water cleanses. Water gives life. God repeatedly used water to save his people throughout history. However, the water of Baptism is special; it has been made holy and gives new life to your child. The baptismal waters wash away original sin, bringing the gift of the Holy Spirit and making your child a part of the body of Christ, the Church. At Baptism, your child receives the living water that leads to a life of mission, meaning, and joy.

3. Oil
In the Old Testament, oil was a sign of God's presence and power on a person. To the early Christians, oil represented how the baptized are sealed with the Holy Spirit of God. When your child is anointed with oil, let it serve as a reminder that the Holy Spirit has come upon your child at Baptism and will be a part of his or her life from now on. This Spirit will give hope to your child in times of despair, encouragement in times of doubt, and confidence in the face of fear.

4. White Garments
Wearing white—a symbol of purity, innocence, and new life—signifies putting on the mantle of Christ. On the day of her Baptism, your child will wear Jesus—talk about "name brand" clothes! As your child grows and receives other sacraments, she will be reminded of this relationship with Jesus by wearing white for First Communion and Confirmation.

5. Sign of the Cross
The world changed at three o'clock on a Friday afternoon when Jesus laid down his life for us on the cross. He took the cross, an instrument of death and torture, and turned it into the means of salvation for us all. At Baptism, the sign of the cross will be traced on your child's forehead. This act boldly declares that she is now a new person, reborn. This gift is a pure grace. We will never be worthy of it, but out of his great love for us, Jesus nonetheless grants us this incredible gift.

Soul Bath

Watch the video, answer the questions to the right,
and discuss additional thoughts.

DynamicCatholic.com/SoulBath

Talk About the Video

What part (or parts) of Baptism excites you most? Why?

What does it mean to you for your child to be adopted by God? Have you ever considered that this is what happens at Baptism?

Think of your godparents. Have they had an active role in your faith formation? How important to you is that your child's godparents are active in his or her life? What can you do to ensure the godparents are as involved as you would like?

Prayer for a Child

Lord,

Why is it that at the most confusing time of our lives we have to learn the most? We have to carry so much within. We must learn to listen. We must listen to learn.

All is decision, all is choice, all is question.

Help my child to find friends who will accept him. Help him to be strong when difficult choices come. Help him to live with values that You value.

When he is anxious, when he is hurting, when he is confused, when he is lazy, when he is troubled, when he is fearful, when he is rejected, when he is ridiculed, when he is moody, when he is misunderstood, be with him, Lord.

When he is happy, when he celebrates, when he wins, when he falls in love, when he passes with flying colors, when he finishes the assignment, when he finds his place, when he belongs, be with him, Lord.

Teach him understanding. Teach him compassion. Teach him empathy. Teach him respect. Teach him graciousness. Teach him forgiveness. Teach him courage, that others will find in him what he longs to be.

On each new day, bless those who love him. Bless those who teach him. Bless those who befriend him. Bless those who accept him. Bless his family, friends, and all who know him.

May all that he has learned be not in vain, for if he has never lost, he will not search again.

Amen.

Four Things

According to the Catechism, "Holy Baptism is the basis of the whole Christian life, the gateway to life in the Spirit *(vitae spiritualis ianua)*, and the door which gives access to the other sacraments. Through Baptism we are freed from sin and reborn as sons of God; we become members of Christ, are incorporated into the Church and made sharers in her mission: 'Baptism is the sacrament of regeneration through water in the word'" (1213).

You may be thinking that sometimes reading the Catechism can feel like reading from a textbook on quantum physics . . . upside down.

But it's actually quite simple. When you have your child baptized, four incredible things happen:

1. Your child becomes a member of the Church.
On the day of his Baptism, your child officially becomes a member of the largest family in the world—the Catholic Church. He is about to gain 1.2 billion new brothers and sisters! And as a member of the Church, your child has access to the other sacraments. Welcome to the family of God!

2. Your child is adopted by God.
Every parent eventually has to come to grips with the reality that they will never be able to fully protect their child from a world filled with violence and suffering. Not only will you be unable to protect her, but your love, despite your best efforts, will occasionally fall short of what she deserves.

But on the day of her Baptism, your child won't just be your daughter. She will become the child of God the Father. She will be the child of the great King!

(See page 17 for one way to remind your child of this each day of her life.)

3. Your child is cleansed of original sin.
We know the things that make us happy, but we don't always do them. We choose lesser things; we opt for a-lesser-version-of-ourselves.

God desires greater things for us. His original plan was for us to be happy with him forever. Adam and Eve chose to disobey God and eat the forbidden fruit because they wanted to be like God (Genesis 3:5). They envisioned a life in which God was not necessary for their happiness. That's the original sin: seeking happiness in ourselves apart from God.

In many ways, original sin acts like a blood clot. Just like a clot prevents life-giving blood from flowing properly in our bodies and can even cause death, original sin clogs our spiritual arteries, preventing the life-giving flow of God's grace and Spirit in us. It cuts us off from life with God. Just like a blood clot, original sin leads to death.

God has great gifts he wants to give us through grace. His powerful grace helps us choose to live the great life he dreams for us. And grace helps us live in heaven with God forever. But like a blood clot, original sin stands in the way of our receiving that gift.

Thankfully, that's where Jesus comes in.

Baptism unleashes the power of Jesus' life, death, resurrection, and ascension in our lives. Jesus became man. He died on the cross to make amends for our sins. He then rose from the dead to liberate us from death, and ascended into heaven to open the way home for us. In other words, Jesus makes it possible for the clot to be healed. He sets us right with God.

Baptism removes the clot and opens the way for God's great gifts to saturate your child's soul now and forever.

4. Your child is sealed with the Holy Spirit.
Your child's forehead is "marked" or "sealed" during his Baptism. Physically, with the anointing of oil, but also spiritually, with the Holy Spirit.

Relatives might give your little girl or boy a card with five dollars in it or a rosary on this wonderful day, but God gives your child the gifts of the Holy Spirit. And what gifts they are! Wisdom, understanding, knowledge, fortitude, piety, counsel, and fear of the Lord. You are choosing these gifts for your child now in Baptism, and he will later make his own choice to strengthen them in Confirmation.

. . .

Pretty good stuff, isn't it?

DISCUSS

Choosing Your Child's Godparents

A godparent assists the parents in passing the Catholic faith on to the child. As a result, only a godparent who supports in both words and actions the child's growth in the faith can fulfill this duty well. It is important to note that only one godparent is required, though traditionally two (a male and a female) are selected. Give this choice some thought. A godparent can have a remarkable influence on your child.

The godparent is required to be:

- at least sixteen years of age (the priest or deacon can make an exception for someone younger as long as the other requirements are fulfilled)
- baptized, confirmed, and has received First Communion
- living a life consistent with the Catholic faith
- an active member of the Catholic Church
- someone other than one of the biological parents

Since only one godparent is required, another person can serve as a "Christian witness," as long as he or she is:

- a baptized Christian in good standing
- the opposite sex of the godparent

Who are your child's godparents, and why did you choose them?

Godmother: ....

Why did you choose this woman?

Godfather: ....

Why did you choose this man?

Letters

Watch the video, answer the questions to the right, and discuss additional thoughts.

DynamicCatholic.com/Letters

Talk About the Video

If you could send a message back through time, what's the ONE THING you would tell the 18-year-old version of yourself?

What's been your favorite part of being a mom or a dad?

Writing Your Vows:

No one asks you to make vows when you have your baby. Well I'm asking you to do that now. Write down some of your vows or promises to your child. Pick out your favorites and work them into your letter (see next page).

Writing Your Letter:

Writer your own letter to give to your child when he or she is 18. You can write in the space provided here and give your child the entire book, or write on a separate page and seal the letter in an envelope for later. Really take your time with it and store it somewhere special so you don't lose it!

READ

Be Not Afraid

Be not afraid. The Scriptures tell us this nearly one hundred times, because Jesus knew the measure of our lives will be the measure of our courage.

Raising great children requires courage. It will take courage to get really intentional with how you raise yours. It will take courage to be countercultural, to raise your child in the Catholic faith, and to pursue the dreams you and God share for your child's life. And it will take courage to strive each day to become a-better-version-of-yourself and challenge your child to do the same.

Be not afraid.

God said it to Abraham, Moses, and Ruth.

The angel said it to Mary, the shepherds, and Zechariah.

Jesus said it to the disciples, the two men on the road to Emmaus, and to Mary Magdalene on Easter Sunday.

Be not afraid.

This is God's message to you and your child on the day of Baptism and on all the days that follow.

Baptism is not an end but a beginning. It is the starting point of a lifelong, joy-filled relationship with God.

Thank you for allowing the Dynamic Catholic team to be with you during this part of your journey. I pray it is the beginning of a dynamic collaboration between you and God to help your child live a great life.

Do not be afraid!

—The Dynamic Catholic Team

HAVE YOU EVER WONDERED HOW THE CATHOLIC FAITH COULD HELP YOU LIVE BETTER?

How it could help you find more *joy* at work, *manage* your personal finances, *improve* your marriage, or make you a *better* parent?

THERE IS GENIUS IN CATHOLICISM.

When *Catholicism* is lived as it is intended to be, it elevates every part of our lives. It may sound simple, but they say *genius is taking something complex and making it simple.*

Dynamic Catholic started with a dream: to help ordinary people discover the *genius of Catholicism.*

Wherever you are in your journey, we want to meet you there and walk with you, *step by step*, helping you to discover God and become *the-best-version-of-yourself.*

To find more helpful resources, visit us online at DynamicCatholic.com.

 Dynamic Catholic

FEED YOUR SOUL.